the me I **want** to be

teen edition

participant's guide

the me I **want** to be

» becoming God's best version of you

teen edition

participant's guide
five sessions

john ortberg
with scott rubin

youth specialties

ZONDERVAN.com/
AUTHORTRACKER
follow your favorite authors

ZONDERVAN

The Me I Want to Be, Teen Edition Participant's Guide
Copyright © 2010 by John Ortberg

YS Youth Specialties is a trademark of YOUTHWORKS!, INCORPORATED and is regis-
tered with the United States Patent and Trademark Office.

Requests for information should be addressed to:

Zondervan, *Grand Rapids, Michigan* 49530

ISBN 978-0-310-67109-1

All Scripture quotations, unless otherwise indicated, are taken from the Holy Bible, *Today's
New International Version®, TNIV®*. Copyright © 2001, 2005 by Biblica, Inc.™ Used by permission of Zondervan. All rights reserved worldwide.

Scripture quotations marked NLT are taken from the *Holy Bible, New Living Translation*, copyright © 1996, 2004. Used by permission of Tyndale House Publishers, Inc., Wheaton, Illinois.
All rights reserved.

Scripture quotations marked MSG are taken from *The Message*. Copyright © 1993, 1994, 1995,
1996, 2000, 2001, 2002. Used by permission of NavPress Publishing Group.

Scripture quotations marked NASB are taken from the *New American Standard Bible*. Copyright © 1960, 1962, 1963, 1968, 1971, 1972, 1973, 1975, 1977, 1995 by The Lockman Foundation.
Used by permission.

*Cover and interior design: Lindsay Lang Sherbondy with Heartland Community Church
Interior design management: Ben Fetterley*

Printed in the United States of America

10 11 12 13 14 15 16 17 /DCI/ 22 21 20 19 18 17 16 15 14 13 12 11 10 9 8 7 6 5 4 3 2 1

contents

Session ONE

Discovering the Spirit

»

Discovering the Spirit

Really Living is never just about you; it's a "so that" kind of thing. In other words, God designed you to Really Live "so that" you could be part of his mission on earth; or God wants you to Really Live "so that" people can be encouraged, gardens can be planted, music can be written, sick people can be helped, and schools can thrive. So when you fail to become the person God designed, all the rest of us miss out on the gift you were made to give!

The Me I Want to Be, Teen Edition, chapter 2

» DVD Notes

As you watch the Session 1 video-teaching segment, take notes in the following section on anything that stands out to you. An outline has been provided so you can follow along.

There is a God...and it's not you. Your life isn't your project...it's God's project.

Really Living means growing the way God designed you to grow...and it means becoming "you-ier."

"Counterfeit" or "fake" versions of me that I sometimes choose:

The "me" I pretend to be	I try to act important or cool, while secretly fearing I'm not.
The "me" I think I should be	I try to be someone I'm not meant to be (and I usually do this because I'm comparing myself to others)
The "me" other people want me to be	I don't feel free to be myself; I feel like I have to follow someone else's plans for me.
The "me" I'm afraid God wants me to be	I don't completely trust in God's love and plan, and sometimes I think being spiritually mature just means following the rules in the Bible.
The "me" that fails to be	I don't feel very excited about life; I'm exhausted and unmotivated.

But the best version of me is...

The "me" I'm meant to be	I feel really alive inside...and I'm growing more like Christ!

God's Best Version of you is always waiting...there's always a next step.

» DVD Group Discussion

1. Of the five kinds of "counterfeit" or "fake me's" listed in the chart on page 10, which one do you most easily act like? Why? What kinds of situations influence you to become that "fake" you?

2. *The Me I Want to Be, Teen Edition* says that God is always guiding you toward the Best Version of you all the time. Can you follow God if you don't trust that God really cares deeply about you and has your best interests at heart? Do you believe these things about God? Why...or why not?

3. *The Me I Want to Be, Teen Edition* talks about how all kinder-
garteners see themselves as artists. But as the years go by, fewer
and fewer think of themselves as artists...as if their dreams were
smothered. Have you known people who've been criticized or
felt judged by others and that criticism or judgment affected their
dreams? Have *you* ever had a dream that was squashed or beaten
down?

4. If someone were to ask you how your spiritual life is going, what
factors would you think about before you answered? What answer
would you give?

The Me I Want to Be, Teen Edition says that a wise man once
suggested that when you're asked, "How is your spiritual life
going?" you should think about these two questions before you
answer:

- Am I more easily discouraged these days?
- Am I more easily irritated these days?

How would you answer these questions today? What do your
answers to these two questions tell you about your spiritual life?

5. Check out the definitions for these two terms:

> REALLY LIVING = being full of joy and peace, in harmony with God, others, self; curious, willing to learn and experience opportunities to grow toward the Best Version of ourselves
>
> DECAYING = lacking mental and emotional energy, feeling uneasy and not very content, self-focused — the opposite of Really Living's characteristics

On a line between REALLY LIVING and DECAYING, mark where you live most of the time:

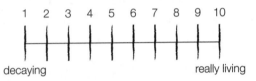

Have you ever thought of yourself as too young or too _____ (fill in the blank) to Really Live—or to grow toward the Best Version of you? Do you need to adjust your thinking here? What adjustments do you need to make?

» Group Bible Exploration

1. Have you ever helped your family do a home improvement project or taken a class at school where you fixed up something? What was the end result? (Take just a minute to share your responses.)

Restoring or fixing something helps us see its original value or beauty more clearly. Read together 2 Corinthians 5:17:

> Therefore, if anyone is in Christ, the new creation has come: The old has gone, the new is here!

Becoming a new creation doesn't mean we become completely different. Instead—as noted in *The Me I Want to Be, Teen Edition*—we are being "restored to [our] intended beauty." What's stopping you from working toward becoming all that God intended you to be? Do you suppose that your "holding back" could affect those around you? How?

2. Read together Psalm 92:12–13:

> The righteous will flourish like a palm tree, they will grow like a cedar of Lebanon; planted in the house of the LORD, they will flourish in the courts of our God.

God is interested in your individual growth. If you were an acorn, God wouldn't want or expect you to become a rosebush or shrub—God designed acorns to become oak trees. Really Living is becoming more of what God made *you* to be. Is there something you're trying to be or do right now that God didn't design you to be or do? Or have you given up on (or stopped pursuing) a dream or goal that God might have given you? What reasons have contributed to your doing something that you're not designed for...or to your *not doing* something that you'd love to do? What's one thing you can do to take a step in the "Really Living" direction?

3. Joy is a gift God gives us when we're flourishing...and in step with the Holy Spirit. Read together 1 Peter 1:8:

> Though you have not seen [Jesus], you love him...and are filled with an inexpressible and glorious joy.

Have you ever experienced this kind of joy or happiness that Peter describes? How do you suppose others would describe your joy factor? What reasons would they have for their answers?

4. Rest—in other words, being relaxed and not super stressed-out—is another piece of becoming who God made you to be. Rest is important enough that even *God* rested after creating the world. And Jesus tells us in Matthew 11:29 that he wants us to carve out times when we rest. Read Jesus' words:

> Take my yoke upon you and learn from me, for I am gentle and humble in heart, and you will find rest for your souls.

What are some ways you rest, chill, and relax...so you can flourish? What things in your schedule or calendar from the last few weeks or months show that you're making time to rest? Or...do you need to make room for some chill time?

5. Okay, close your eyes for a minute. (But read these next two sentences before you do!) Imagine that you're wandering in the desert and desperately need some water. What words would you use to describe your feelings upon finding that water? (Okay—now you can close your eyes.)

Open your eyes and read together Psalm 42:1:

> As the deer pants for streams of water,
> so my soul pants for you, my God.

Why do you suppose the writer of this psalm chose this word picture to illustrate how much he desires God? Think for a moment: Have you ever experienced this desperate, I-really-really-really-need-God kind of desire? What could you do to grow your desire to know God more deeply?

» In Closing

As you finish your group time, pray together. Ask God to help every member of your group figure out which "fake me's" they sometimes become, then ask God to help each person take steps to flourish and become the "me" God intended. Pray for everyone to hear God's promptings in their lives this week—and that they'd have the courage to follow them.

Before your next meeting, complete the "On Your Own Between Sessions" section (pages 18–19). Then start your next meeting by having everyone share what they learned from this exercise.

»On Your Own Between Sessions

Look back at the chart on page 10. On a piece of paper or in a journal—or maybe in a notebook you bring to school—create a chart listing the possible "counterfeit" or "fake me" options. (Check out the example below.) Over the next few days, keep that chart handy and monitor your "me-ness" by checkmarking the "counterfeit me's" that you become in different situations. Try to jot down some notes about what might have influenced you to act the way you did. After a few days, ask yourself if you see any patterns or habits in your behavior.

CHART EXAMPLE:

Counterfeit/ Fake Me Options	How Often This Week?	Notes
The "me" I pretend to be	✓ ✓ ✓ ✓	I start doing this every time I'm around 'popular' people. Why does being on the team make me feel like pretending to be so cool?
The "me" I think I should be	✓	Why does it stress me out SO bad that I'm not getting all As?
The "me" other people want me to be	✓ ✓	Whenever my dad starts talking about my future, I get all concerned that I'm not living up to what he wants.
The "me" I'm afraid God wants me to be	✓ ✓ ✓	I'm scared to trust God when I sense God wants me to talk to the quiet kid in my class; what if people make fun of me?
The "me" that fails to be	✓	I'm so tired—practice for the team and everything else I'm doing takes so much time; homework keeps me up late.

After you've filled in your chart for a few days, try to look at it through God's eyes. Can you see where you're trying to be or do something that God isn't asking you to be or do? Are there areas where you can be more "in the flow of the Spirit"—listening and following through on what the Holy Spirit is telling you to do (or not do)? Do you see areas where it would feel freeing to become the "you" that God truly made you to be?

In *The Message* version of the Bible, Paul writes, "Rule-keeping does not naturally evolve into living by faith, but only perpetuates itself in more and more rule-keeping" (Galatians 3:12). Closing the gap between being less "fake" and more like the "you" God made you to be doesn't come from following the rules...or trying harder to be good. The size of that gap can only lessen through God's grace and by listening to the Holy Spirit—following through on the Holy Spirit's guidance. And when you mess up, you need to give yourself grace and take a fresh start.

As you think back on this exercise, what are two specific ways that you can better battle the temptation to become a "fake me" and instead move toward becoming the "me you were meant to be"?

1.

2.

» Recommended Reading

In preparation for Session 2, you may want to read chapters 6 through 9 of *The Me I Want to Be, Teen Edition*. To review what you studied in Session 1, you may want to read chapters 1 through 5 of the book also.

Session TWO

Renewing My Mind

»

Renewing My Mind

Becoming the best version of yourself, then, rests on one simple instruction: *Think great thoughts!* People who live great lives are people who habitually think great thoughts. Their thoughts move them toward confidence, love, and joy. Trying to change your emotions by willpower alone and without allowing the stream of your thoughts to be changed by the flow of the Spirit is like disinfecting the house of the skunk smell while the skunks are still living in your basement. But God can change the way we think.

The Me I Want to Be, Teen Edition, chapter 7

» DVD Notes

As you watch the Session 2 video-teaching segment, take notes in the following section on anything that stands out to you. An outline has been provided for you to follow along.

There's no power like "got-to-have" desires and dreams.

As you open yourself to the flow of the Spirit, you start to love God more and more—not because you *should*, but because you can't help it. And this changes your desires.

True change always begins in the mind. So becoming the Best Version of you is based on thinking great thoughts.

You must learn to take charge of and set your mind. You have the freedom to choose what you pay attention to.

» DVD Group Discussion

1. Do you generally view desires as *positive* or *negative*? Did you ever think of your desires as being God's gift to you—part of God's creative design?

When you're able to satisfy one of your God-given desires (for example, creating a piece of art or music, serving or helping somebody, being outside in nature), how do you feel? How do you suppose this makes God feel?

Do temptations toward "bad stuff" lessen at all when your God-given desires are satisfied? Why?

2. We all have likes and dislikes. What are some things that register high on your "like-o-meter"? What kinds of stuff hit the low spots? Why does it even matter what you like and dislike?

3. We can put most earthly desires into four categories: Material (in other words, stuff), Achievement and Accomplishment, Relational, and Physical. In the chart on page 26, jot down your desire factor for each of these. Then consider how you could connect those desires back to God. Finally, think about how this desire of yours

could become negative. For example, if you have a high degree of desire for achievement (say, a 5), then you can thank God for your ability to get things done. But you must also realize that if you focus *too much* on achieving, then you may hurt your relationships in the process. (As you complete this chart, remember that these categories aren't necessarily "good" or "bad.")

Desire	My Degree of Desire 1 = Low 5 = High	How can I connect this desire back to God?	How could this desire become negative?
Material (in other words, stuff)			
Achievement and Accomplishment			
Relational			
Physical			

Learning to "connect the dots" between God and the gifts we've been given is a conscious decision. What are some things you can do each day to increase your gratitude for God and God's blessings? (For example, start each day with a prayer of thanks, put notes where you can seem them every day to remind you of God's goodness.)

4. *The Me I Want to Be, Teen Edition* says that our individual spiritual growth requires moving our life with God from "should" (for instance, I should talk with God more, I should read my Bible more) to "want to." Is your relationship with God leaning more toward "should" or "want to"? Why? Do you "like" God right now? How do you feel about where you are?

5. Two people in the same *situation* can have very different *experiences* because of their individual ways of thinking. (For example, one may see something as a problem; the other may see it as an opportunity.) Consider your own thought life. Do your thoughts tend to be more positive or more negative?

If you want to change the way you think—to move more toward God—then you must start by learning to take charge of your mind. Do you really believe that you have the ability not only to influence, but actually *change* your thought patterns? Why or why not?

6. As we learn to take control of our thoughts, we must next learn to set our minds—decide what we'll think about. *The Me I Want to Be, Teen Edition* says that to "think great thoughts" is to have thoughts that move us toward things such as confidence, love, and joy—toward God. It's like creating a target to shoot for in our minds. Right now, assess your ability to regularly "think great thoughts" by marking how often you're able to do it on the following line:

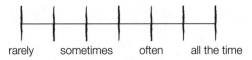

rarely   sometimes   often   all the time

How can you increase your habit of "great thought" thinking?

7. *Freedom* can mean different things to different people. What freedom is important to you personally (for instance, deciding whom to hang out with, choosing how to spend your down time)?

What freedom do you have when it comes to your mind and thoughts?

The Evil One is waging a spiritual battle against you and your thoughts. How much control do you have in this battle? What is the danger—to you and to those around you—if you choose *not* to monitor your thought life?

8. In order to think great thoughts, we need life-giving fuel. One of the best possible tools in our thought life is God's Word. God loves us whether or not we read the Bible, but God has given us the gift of Scripture to help us grow! Without feeling guilty about your response, how often do you read your Bible? What reasons affect your answer? What's a practical, specific action you can take to read the Bible with curiosity on a more regular basis?

» Group Bible Exploration

1. Think back over your thought life from the past several days. How would you generally describe the trend or pattern of your thoughts (for example, positive, discouraged, worried)? Were you aware of the kinds of thought patterns you had?

Read together 2 Corinthians 10:5:

> We demolish arguments and every pretension that sets itself up against the knowledge of God, and we take captive every thought to make it obedient to Christ.

Is it a common practice for you to take all your thoughts to God, as the Bible tells us to do? What makes that hard—or easy—for you to do?

2. You may have heard the phrase "garbage in, garbage out." When you consider your thought life, were there times this week that you allowed "garbage in" or consciously allowed yourself to have thoughts you knew you shouldn't let in? Share a brief example (if you're bold enough), or maybe share about the kinds of thoughts that fall under this category of "garbage in."

Read together all of Psalm 139, if time permits. It's such a cool chapter. If you don't have enough time, then read together these summary verses:

You have searched me, LORD, and you know me.... All the days ordained for me were written in your book before one of them came to be.... Search me, God, and know my heart; test me and know my anxious thoughts. (vv. 1, 16, 23)

If God already knows the thoughts of King David (who wrote this psalm), why does David invite God to search his thinking?

What's the benefit of bringing our "offensive ways" (see verse 24) to our awareness and to God's? What role might forgiveness play in allowing us to Really Live—or to grow more into the Best Version of ourselves?

3. Read together the following Scriptures:

> Those who live according to the sinful nature have their minds set on what that nature desires; but those who live in accordance with the Spirit have their minds set on what the Spirit desires. The mind controlled by the sinful nature is death, but the mind controlled by the Spirit is life and peace. The sinful mind is hostile to God; it does not submit to God's law, nor can it do so. Those controlled by the sinful nature cannot please God. (Romans 8:5–8)
>
> Since, then, you have been raised with Christ, set your hearts on things above, where Christ is seated at the right hand of God. Set your minds on things above, not on earthly things. (Colossians 3:1–2)
>
> Do not conform to the pattern of this world, but be transformed by the renewing of your mind. (Romans 12:2)

What's the common theme in these passages? How would you define "set your minds"? How do you determine what to set your mind on—what kinds of thoughts to think about?

In what direction will your thoughts lead you when you're controlled by the Spirit? What kinds of thoughts do you have if you're controlled by your sinful nature—by "the pattern of this world"?

As you think about these passages, what do you hear the Holy Spirit nudging or prompting you to do in your own life? Ask the Holy Spirit to really speak to you.

4. Read together the following Scriptures:

> So Jacob served seven years to get Rachel [as his wife], but they seemed like only a few days to him because of his love for her. (Genesis 29:20)
>
> "The kingdom of heaven is like treasure hidden in a field. When a man found it, he hid it again, and then in his joy went and sold all he had and bought that field. Again, the kingdom of heaven is like a merchant looking for fine pearls. When he found one of great value, he went away and sold everything he had and bought it." (Matthew 13:44–46)

What desire did these three guys (Jacob, the man, and the merchant) all share?

Have you ever experienced this kind of desire—or dream—for something? Use single words (for instance, *excitement, fear*) to tell the group what kinds of feelings you had when you were in pursuit of your desire or dream.

Have you ever considered where your desires come from? Are they related to your passions or gifts?

5. Check out this passage from *The Me I Want to Be, Teen Edition*:

> Spiritual growth doesn't mean a life spent doing what I *should* do instead of what I *want* to do. It means getting to the point where I want to do what I should do. When people come to understand how good God is, they *want* him. They don't just love him. They *like* him.
>
> The "ought" of Jesus' message is mainly an ought of opportunity.
>
> When we become aware of this, we feel guilty because our desire for God does not run deep enough — but we can't make ourselves desire God more by telling ourselves that we should. God is so gracious and patient, waiting for us to want him; and God is glad to work with this kind of honesty. That is why we are invited to "taste and see that the LORD is good."
>
> *Taste* is an experimental word. It is an invitation from a confident chef. You don't have to commit to eating the whole thing; just try a sample — a *taste*. If you don't like it, you can skip the rest. But the chef is convinced that if you can be persuaded to take one bite, you'll want the whole enchilada.

Do you sometimes struggle with *wanting* to desire God? If so, how do you picture God responding toward you in that struggle?

Read together Psalm 34:8:

> Taste and see that the LORD is good; blessed are those who take refuge in him.

Does this verse change your perspective on God's heart toward you? What do you think it means to taste and see that the Lord is good? Can enjoying all that God created help you to taste and see that the Lord is good? How?

Read together James 1:17:

> Every good and perfect gift is from above, coming down from the Father of the heavenly lights, who does not change like shifting shadows.

How could your growing desire for God be connected to receiving enjoyment from the good gifts in your life?

» In Closing

Pray together as you end this session. Ask God to help the group members be willing to look deeply at their own desires and thought lives and allow God to fully search their hearts. Pray for wisdom in seeing where God is leading you to turn your desires toward God.

Before you meet again, complete the following "On Your Own Between Sessions" section beginning on page 36. Then consider starting the next session by sharing what group members learned from this individual exercise.

» On Your Own Between Sessions

Thinking great thoughts can be kind of hard to understand and do. How motivated are you to do the work it may require to both take control of your thinking and set your mind consistently on the presence and goodness of God—to move toward God more and more in your thought life? If you're up to the challenge (and we believe you are!), do this "on your own" exercise.

1. Start by asking God to search you and uncover your blind spots—places of sin in your life that you aren't aware of (see again Psalm 139:23–24). Review the past day or two. Can you recognize any common thought patterns that aren't honoring to you or to God? For example, do you focus on the negatives in your life too often? Do you have a critical spirit toward others or find fault with them too easily? Do you often cut short your time with God and your Bible reading to do something else?

   If you're having trouble identifying your thought patterns (and you're feeling brave), ask a few close friends to share what they've observed in you lately. Then, as a first step in thinking great thoughts, confess any thought patterns you find that don't honor God. Note them here:

2. Next, think again about Romans 12:2—"Let God transform you into a new person by changing the way you think" (NLT). Then ask God to prepare you to take steps of growth. Go ahead—ask! Write your prayer here, if you want to:

3. Philippians 4:8 says, "Whatever is noble, whatever is right, whatever is pure, whatever is lovely, whatever is admirable—if anything is excellent or praiseworthy—think about such things." This offers clear-cut direction on thinking great thoughts. Using these categories (noble, lovely, pure, and so on), make a list of things in your life that fit into them (for instance, a friendship, a hobby you love, something that God's blessed you with).

4. Beginning right now, take a "snapshot" of your thoughts on a regular basis for the rest of the day. Maybe you can set your watch or phone to go off every couple of hours. When the alarm rings, consider the kind of thought pattern you're in right then. If you find that you aren't thinking a Philippians 4:8 kind of thought, ask God to help you exchange it for something on your list. As the day winds down, try to identify the non-Philippians 4:8 kinds of thoughts you had.

5. Ask God to increase your awareness of this thought battle you're engaged in every day. And for the next week, consider letting your watch or phone timer ring regularly to remind you to think great

thoughts. Finally, choose just one specific thing you'll do to grow in changing the way you think. Write it here as a reminder...and consider sharing it with a friend who can help keep you on track:

» Recommended Reading

In preparation for Session 3, you may want to read chapters 10 through 13 of *The Me I Want to Be, Teen Edition.*

Session THREE
Redeeming My Time
»

Redeeming My Time

We become vulnerable to temptation when we are dissatisfied with our lives. The deeper our dissatisfaction, the deeper our vulnerability...because we were made for soul satisfaction. We can't live without it. If we don't find soul satisfaction in God, we'll look for it somewhere else.

The Me I Want to Be, Teen Edition, chapter 11

» DVD Notes

As you watch the Session 3 video-teaching segment, take notes in the following section on anything that stands out to you. An outline has been provided so you can follow along.

The goal of prayer is to live life and speak all our words in the fantastic awareness of God's presence.

Problems and temptations try to keep us out of life in the flow of the Spirit...but we can use them to remind us to pray.

The Spirit moves us toward forgiveness, redemption, and healing.

The pattern of our sin is related to the pattern of our passion, wiring, and gifts.

» DVD Group Discussion

1. Think about talking with a really close friend. How do you usually feel when you're in that conversation? Now shift your focus to praying—talking with God the Father. How do you feel when you're in *that* conversation? Is it easy or challenging for you to think of conversation (prayer) with God as being like a conversation with a close friend? If you're feeling satisfied by God, do you tend to feel closer to God when you pray?

2. How would you answer if someone asked, "How is your prayer life going?" What factors do you consider? How would you answer that question right now?

Why do you suppose God allows you to sometimes feel far away from him when you pray? How often do you believe sin plays a role in not feeling God's presence?

3. Have you ever thought that lack of self-awareness could be dangerous? *The Me I Want to Be, Teen Edition* says: "One of the most common areas where people can end up fooling themselves is their spiritual lives. How many of us have given serious thought to how our lives would grade out—not by the standard of the neighborhood sandlot where we can always find a first-grader to outperform, but in the eyes of a holy, rightous, and truth-telling God?" Why is deceiving ourselves or justifying our actions so concerning? Do you suppose it's easier to see this dishonesty in your own life, or in others' lives? How can you increase your self-awareness?

4. *The Me I Want to Be, Teen Edition* says that the pattern of our sin is related to the pattern of our gifts. It goes on to discuss nine common personality types and their corresponding sin patterns. Take a few minutes to read through this information on pages 44–48; as you do, try to evaluate what your own personality type may be.

Personality Types: Their Strengths and Weaknesses*

Reformer

Strengths	• Lives with an internal standard of what is good, noble, and beautiful • Calls others to live better lives
Weaknesses	• Can be arrogant when unredeemed • Has high standards that can lead to a secret, inner sense of inadequacy
Example	The prophet Amos, who showed Israel the standard God expected of society
My Notes**	

Server

Strengths	• Practices love in action • Has a natural concern for others that makes people feel cared for
Weaknesses	• Can use "giving" to manipulate other people • Sometimes equates servanthood with fear or low esteem
Example	Martha, who was busy serving while her sister, Mary, sat at Jesus' feet
My Notes**	

---

* Summarized from Michael Mangis' book *Signature Sins: Taming Our Wayward Hearts* (InterVarsity Press, 2008).
** To be used in the "On Your Own Between Sessions" section.

Achiever

Strengths
- Has a strong desire to grow
- Has the ability to accomplish things and add value in the lives and world around them

Weaknesses
- Has the temptation to be preoccupied with one's own success
- Sometimes uses other people to receive applause or approval

Example
Solomon, who sought achievement in education, finance, culture, and the arts

My Notes**

Artist

Strengths
- Loves beauty and goodness
- Brings imagination to life, love, and faith

Weaknesses
- Discovers that being different can become an end in itself
- Can be tempted to give in to impulses and live an undisciplined life

Example
King David, who had strong gifts as a poet, dancer, and composer of many psalms

My Notes**

Thinker

Strengths
- Is a discoverer, inventor, and lover of logic
- Holds a passion for truth — even when it's costly

Weaknesses
- The conviction of being "right" can lead to arrogance
- Can be tempted to withdraw from relationships and love

Example
The apostle Paul, who loved to study, reason, explore, and teach

My Notes**

Loyalist

Strengths
- Is faithful and dependable when the chips are down
- Loves to be part of a great team

Weaknesses
- Is prone to skepticism or cynicism
- When threatened, can be pushed into isolation by fear

Example
Elisha, who became Elijah's steadfast companion

My Notes**

Enthusiast

Strengths
- Has high capacity for joy and emotional expression
- Has enthusiasm that is contagious for others

Weaknesses
- May need to be the center of attention
- May avoid pain, which can lead to escape or addiction

Example
The apostle Peter, who was the first one to leap out of the boat — even if it meant sinking

My Notes**

Commander

Strengths
- Has a passion for justice and a desire to champion a great cause
- Has the personality to lead (which inspires others)

Weaknesses
- May seek power that can cause others to feel used
- Sometimes relies on fear and intimidation to get results

Example
Nehemiah, who was moved to action — rallying followers and defying opponents — when he heard Jerusalem was in ruins

My Notes**

Peacemaker

Strengths	• Has a natural ability to listen well and give wise counsel
	• Has an easygoing, low-maintenance relational style
Weaknesses	• May smooth things over and avoid conflict
	• Is sometimes passive
Example	Abraham, who was a peacemaker with his wife, his nephew Lot, and foreign leaders — even tried to mediate between God and Sodom and Gomorrah
My Notes**	

Do you see yourself as one personality type or a combination of two or three? What strengths do you possess? Any strength can become a weakness when it's taken too far. Do you agree with the weaknesses connected to your personality type(s)?

5. *The Me I Want to Be, Teen Edition* says, "We aren't tempted by stuff that disgusts us." If that's true, do you suppose that awareness of your personality type can help you guard against temptation? How?

6. How important to you are each of the following options whenever you face temptation? (Ranking Scale: 1 = Not at all important, 3 = Somewhat important, 5 = Very important)

   • Having decided (ahead of time) on the kind of person you want to become and why

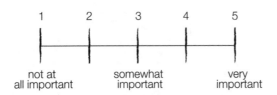

   • Asking for help from a friend (not being isolated from community)

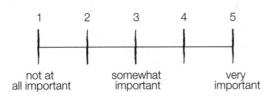

- Asking yourself, *Where will this thought or decision lead me?*

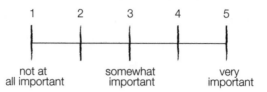

not at
all important   somewhat
important   very
important

- Staying aware of how satisfied your soul is feeling (and making any necessary adjustments) so sin doesn't look good to you

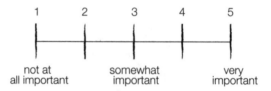

not at
all important   somewhat
important   very
important

- Moving toward God when you do sin

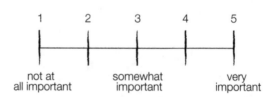

not at
all important   somewhat
important   very
important

- Other _____

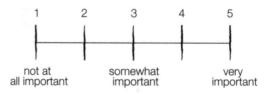

not at
all important   somewhat
important   very
important

At this point in your life, which one or two of these actions would be the most helpful to you in battling temptation?

7. Our souls are meant to be satisfied by God; that's God's design and desire. How do you measure how your soul—or heart—is doing? Why is it important for us to keep watch over the conditions of our souls? When you're experiencing soul *dis*satisfaction, what does that look like for you personally? What helps you most in keeping your soul connected to God—in other words, desiring God and resisting temptation?

8. When you do sin (because all of us do), how easy is it for you to receive forgiveness from God? Why does it matter that you receive forgiveness? What do you suppose can happen to your soul if you carry around the weight of something for which you've not been forgiven? How does your receiving *and* offering forgiveness affect you and those with whom you're in community?

» Group Bible Exploration

1. *The Me I Want to Be, Teen Edition* says that being *with* another person influences the words we say (in other words, we might say different things to or about others when they're with us, as opposed to if they aren't around); we tend to "filter" our words. But God reminds us that we can't do this with him—God is *never* absent from us.

   Read together Psalm 139:7–8:

   > Where can I go from your Spirit? Where can I flee from your presence? If I go up to the heavens, you are there; if I make my bed in the depths, you are there.

   When you're pondering something or sharing your thoughts with others, how aware are you that God is always listening to and invested in you? How do you feel about God's constant presence?

   Read this spoken prayer of Jesus from John 11:41–42, which he said right before he raised Lazarus from the dead:

   > "Father, I thank you that you have heard me. I knew that you always hear me, but I said this for the benefit of the people standing here, that they may believe that you sent me."

Close your eyes and picture yourself as a bystander watching this scene. Can you hear Jesus' words? Imagine him talking to the dead man's sister, Martha, in one sentence and then talking to God in the next. Jesus talked with the Father so much that it was an ongoing conversation. What would it take for you to become more conversational with God?

2. To get in the flow of the Spirit, we must be willing to talk to God—to pray—about anything and everything in our lives. When we come to God, we mustn't hide our hearts but offer to God whatever we have: Problems, questions, temptations, thoughts, gratitude, and requests.

Read together Luke 11:10–13:

Don't bargain with God. Be direct. Ask for what you need. This is not a cat-and-mouse, hide-and-seek game we're in. If your little boy asks for a serving of fish, do you scare him with a live snake on his plate? If your little girl asks for an egg, do you trick her with a spider? As bad as you are, you wouldn't think of such a thing—you're at least decent to your own children. And don't you think the Father who conceived you in love will give the Holy Spirit when you ask him? (*The Message*)

What does this verse say about God's heart toward you—and your requests?

What's the easiest thing for you to pray about? Why?

What's the most challenging thing to pray about? Be as specific as you can.

Do you wonder if there are things you should *not* pray about? Explain.

3. Facing temptation can trigger us to pray. Read together James 4:7–10:

> So let God work his will in you. Yell a loud no to the Devil and watch him scamper. Say a quiet yes to God and he'll be there in no time. Quit dabbling in sin. Purify your inner life. Quit playing the field. Hit bottom, and cry your eyes out. The fun and games are over. Get serious, really serious. Get down on your knees before the Master; it's the only way you'll get on your feet. (*The Message*)

In this passage from James, do you see a passive or aggressive response in the face of temptation? Explain.

On a scale of 1 to 10 (1 = Lazy or casual; 5 = Depends on the temptation; 10 = Extremely urgent), how serious are your efforts in resisting temptation? Does reading the Scripture, and then plotting your effort on the continuum here, motivate you to do anything differently when you face temptation?

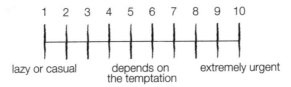

4. Look up Matthew 6:9 – 13, the "Lord's Prayer." Even though you're probably familiar with it, try to read it as though you're reading it for the very first time. What kinds of things does Jesus include in his prayer?

Now read together 1 Thessalonians 5:17 – 18:

> Pray continually, give thanks in all circumstances; for this is God's will for you in Christ Jesus.

If you were to pray in the way this passage instructs, how would that change your prayers? Does it seem possible to change? Does remembering that God is always present make any difference?

The Bible provides many other insights for our prayer lives. On your own, you may want to look up the word *pray* in a concordance and jot down some thoughts on what you read.

5. First Thessalonians 5:19 (in different versions) warns us not to *put out* (New International Version), *stifle* (New Living Translation), *suppress* (*The Message*), or *quench* (King James Version) the Holy Spirit in our lives. What makes you ignore or suppress the Holy Spirit's nudging in your life? When are you most open to the Spirit's work in your life?

Read together the apostle Paul's words in 1 Corinthians 10:13:

No temptation has overtaken you except what is common to us all. And God is faithful; he will not let you be tempted beyond what you can bear. But when you are tempted, he will also provide a way out so that you can endure it.

Have you ever wondered if God can actually relate to your temptations? How does this verse make you feel about God's understanding of your struggles?

Do you ever struggle to believe that you can grow stronger while facing temptations in your life? How does this Scripture affect those thoughts?

» In Closing

As you finish your study today, pray together, asking God to help the members of your group to grow in their ability to talk to God continually throughout the day—about everything.

Pray for openness to the Holy Spirit as each person faces temptations.

And ask God to give all of you the courage to deal with your own pattern of sin—to grow in awareness of and resistance toward it—and to keep moving toward staying in the flow of the Spirit.

Before you move on to Session 4, complete the "On Your Own Between Sessions" section beginning on page 59. Consider starting the next meeting by sharing what each group member learned from this individual exercise.

≫On Your Own Between Sessions

During Session 3's group discussion time, you worked with Michael Mangis' Personality Types chart on pages 44–48. Find that chart again and this time use the "My Notes" section (or the space below, or your journal) to jot down your thoughts about the following exercise.

1. With a desire to increase your self-awareness, think about this past week. Where have you given in to weakness (in thoughts, words, or actions) and moved out of the flow of the Spirit? Based on where and when this happened, can you see any patterns?

2. Is there anyone you need to ask to forgive you if your temptation resulted in sin?

3. Before you're tempted by your sin pattern again, which of the following do you feel motivated to try?
   - Deciding (ahead of time) on the kind of person you want to become and why
   - Asking for help from a friend (not being isolated from community)
   - Asking yourself, *Where will this thought or decision lead me?*
   - Staying aware of how satisfied your soul is feeling (and making any necessary adjustments) so sin doesn't look good to you
   - Moving toward God when you do sin
   - Other _____

After you've considered these insights, talk to God about your thoughts. Ask God to strengthen your determination and give you courage to grow in your desire for God instead of your desire for sin.

» Recommended Reading

In preparation for Session 4, you may want to read chapters 14 through 17 of *The Me I Want to Be, Teen Edition.*

Session FOUR
Deepening My Relationships
»

Deepening My Relationships

A wise man once said that just as the three laws of real estate are "location, location, location," the three laws of relationship are "observation, observation, observation." People who give life to us are people who actually notice us. They know what we love and fear. When we work to really notice someone else, love for that person grows. When we work to really notice someone else, our souls Really Live.

The Me I Want to Be, Teen Edition, chapter 15

» DVD Notes

As you watch the Session 4 video-teaching segment, take notes in the following section on anything that stands out to you. An outline has been provided for you to follow along.

Life-giving relationships need to be a top priority in your life. You Really Live when you're connected to God and his people.

Living in isolation can easily lead to problems such as depression, anxiety, temptation, discouragement, and more.

Identify life-giving people in your world—and be around them!

Connectedness brings the gifts of:
Delight (through serving others you're blessed)

Commitment (to connectedness)

Love (and opportunities to show love)

Belonging (to community)

≫DVD Group Discussion

1. The book notes that the three most important laws of relationship might be called "observation, observation, observation." What does that mean to you? How do you feel when someone truly notices or remembers something about you? Identify some loving people in your life. How do life-giving people affect your heart (versus someone who drains you emotionally)?

   If observation is so important in friendship, what can you do to increase your observation skills toward others? How can it change your focus when you start to observe others more deeply?

2. How connected you feel with God and his people will influence whether you feel more like you're Really Living...or you're Decaying (alone and empty). Where would you put yourself on that scale right now?

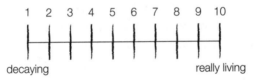

   What situations in your life tend to pull you toward Really Living? Which ones pull you toward Decaying?

3. Why is your commitment to community—to relationships—so important to your spiritual life? Share some specific ways you've been impacted by community. Why do you suppose it's so important that the church gets "community" right?

4. Describe one specific way that you *received* any kind of loving action from someone this week.

Now describe one specific way that you *gave* the gift of love to someone this week. Did you miss any opportunities to love? Did you notice your missed opportunity when it happened, or did you realize it later? What runs through your mind about the missed opportunity?

5. Why do people work so hard to find a sense of belonging—even if it means belonging to something destructive (for instance, a gang or bad friendships)? Does anyone desire the gift of belonging from you, but you haven't given it to them? What's stopping you? What are some simple ways you can choose to help others feel as though they belong—like they have value?

» Group Bible Exploration

1. Just as a new tree needs its roots nourished and room in the ground for it to spread and grow, God says the growth of our spiritual "roots" matters immensely. Look up and read together part of the apostle Paul's awesome prayer in Ephesians 3:17–18:

> And I pray that you, being rooted and established in love, may have power, together with all the Lord's people, to grasp how wide and long and high and deep is the love of Christ.

What does Paul specifically coach Christ-followers to be rooted in? What are some ways we can grow our spiritual roots?

2. Read together Hebrews 10:24 – 25:

> Let us consider how we may spur one another on toward love and good deeds, not giving up meeting together, as some are in the habit of doing, but encouraging one another.

Why does a commitment to community and relationships matter to our individual spiritual health? What's the advantage of regularly being together with other believers?

Check out this passage from *The Me I Want to Be, Teen Edition*:

> Every day, everyone you know faces life with eternity on the line, and life has a way of beating people down. Every life needs a cheering section. Every life needs a shoulder to lean on once in a while. Every life needs prayer. Every life needs a hug sometimes. Every life needs to hear a voice saying, "Don't give up."

What adjustments, if any, do you need to make in your life to receive on a regular basis the gift of community—the kind of encouragement mentioned in the noted passage?

3. Read together the following verses:

> "By this everyone will know that you are my disciples, if you love one another." (John 13:35)
>
> Love must be sincere. Hate what is evil; cling to what is good. Be devoted to one another in brotherly love. Honor one another above yourselves. (Romans 12:9–10)

The Me I Want to Be, Teen Edition, talks about giving and receiving the gift of love when you're in life-giving relationships. How can loving someone help *you* experience more love? What kind of person do you become when you love people?

First John 3:14 says that anyone "who does not love abides in death" (NASB). If you choose to be unloving, what's your attitude likely to be toward temptation or being in the flow of the Spirit?

4. The Bible has a lot to say about joy, which we can also get when we're in life-giving relationships. Do you suppose joy differs from happiness? How would you describe it?

Read the following Scriptures:

"The joy of the LORD is your strength." (Nehemiah 8:10)

Satisfy us in the morning with your unfailing love, that we may sing for joy and be glad all our days. (Psalm 90:14)

Light in a messenger's eyes brings joy to the heart, and good news gives health to the bones. (Proverbs 15:30)

So the women hurried away from [Jesus'] tomb, afraid yet filled with joy, and ran to tell his disciples. (Matthew 28:8)

Why does joy matter in our lives, according to these verses?

» In Closing

As you close this session, pray together, asking God to help each group member not only *seek* life-giving relationships but *provide* them to others. Ask God to help each person receive the gifts of Delight, Commitment, Love, Joy, and Belonging through God-honoring relationships.

And if there are places where group members aren't receiving the gifts that come from connectedness, ask God to provide opportunities for new relationships and growth.

Before moving on to Session 5, complete the "On Your Own Between Sessions" section beginning on page 72. Consider starting the next meeting by having group members share what they learned from this individual exercise.

≫ On Your Own Between Sessions

The Me I Want to Be, Teen Edition says, "When you are loved, it's not just that you get more from someone else—you also become more yourself. *You-ier.* Love brings the power to become the me I want to be. Loving people are literally life-givers. That's connectedness."

Because you're made in God's image, you're designed to be in relationship with others. And it's in relationships where you can Really Live and become more like the Best Version of you! This week, evaluate how connected you are to life-giving relationships. Start by answering the following questions in the Connectedness Inventory.

Connectedness Inventory

Yes	*No*	When something goes wrong, do I have at least one friend I can easily and honestly talk to about it?
Yes	*No*	Is there a friend's home I can go to if I need a break from my own home?
Yes	*No*	Is there someone who really knows my biggest fears and temptations?
Yes	*No*	Do I know the biggest fears and temptations of one or more of my friends?
Yes	*No*	Do I have a friend I trust to keep private the things I share?
Yes	*No*	If I receive good news — like making the team or getting a good grade — do I have a friend I could call right away because I want to share my news?

Think about this exercise and the previous sessions' discussions you've had with your small group. Then respond to the following questions and thoughts.

Who knows you well? Do you have relationships that have the potential to become life-giving relationships (where you feel as though you're fully known and loved no matter what)?

Take some time right now to talk to God about those potential relationships. Is there something God is asking you to do with one of those friendships—like maybe spend some time together and tell them what you're thinking about?

You can be loved best when you're fully known—willing to take off the mask and share who you really are. To be fully known takes courage—and the right kind of friendship. James 5:16 says, "Confess your sins to each other and pray for each other so that you may be healed." Sharing and confessing your sin with a trusted friend can be super-challenging, but also freeing...and healing. Do you have someone in your life with whom you can experience deep sharing—even confession and healing?

Finally, when you think about how connected you feel to others, how often do you experience the following gifts in those relationships? In the blank after each word, enter a 1 (Often), 2 (Sometimes), or 3 (Rarely).

Delight = _____

Commitment = _____

Love = _____

Belonging = _____

If you gave yourself mostly 1s and 2s, congratulations on paying attention to life-giving relationships! But if you answered mostly 2s and 3s, don't give up! Ask God to show you areas where you need to grow in relationship building and to help you experience God's gifts through friendships.

Close your "On Your Own" time with a prayer of thanks for God's gifts—the ones you have right now, as well as those God has in store for you.

» Recommended Reading

In preparation for Session 5, you may want to read chapters 18 and 19 of *The Me I Want to Be, Teen Edition.*

Session FIVE

Transforming My Experience

»

Transforming My Experience

We can't grow apart from challenges to what's familiar and comfortable to us. The Spirit leads us into adventure. The Spirit leads us into a dangerous world. To ask for the Spirit is to ask for risk.

The Me I Want to Be, Teen Edition, chapter 19

» DVD Teaching Notes

As you watch the Session 5 video-teaching segment, take notes in the following section on anything that stands out to you. An outline has been provided so you can follow along.

Companies look for logos that communicate things like success, smarts, pleasure, and power. The cross is like a "logo" that means sacrificial love.

Ask for a challenge bigger than yourself.

You'll know *your* mountain because it'll tap into your greatest strengths and deepest passions.

» DVD Group Discussion

1. *The Me I Want to Be, Teen Edition* talks about companies' logos—that they're carefully chosen to express a certain message (for instance, knowledge, power, success). Can you name a few familiar logos and what you think they represent? If you were to choose a logo for your life (other than the cross), what would it be and why?

   What message does the logo of the cross convey to you?

2. *The Me I Want to Be, Teen Edition* says that we sometimes wish we had problem-free lives, but that kind of life would actually be death by boredom. Do you believe that? Do you tend to look at challenges you face as positives or negatives? Is it tough for you to see challenges as positive?

What are some of the challenges you faced this past week, and what was your typical response to them? (For example, were you energized, irritated, patient, or impatient?) Why?

3. In the story of Granny Brand, we heard about a woman who lived out the statement, "Life is not about comfort." If it's true that we learn and grow best when our comfort is challenged, could this influence your perspective on situations you're facing right now? What might help you respond to these situations with an attitude that's more in the flow of the Spirit?

What emotions do you feel when you consider the fact that God wants to use YOU to tackle a specific "mountain"?

4. Think of a time when you were faced with a challenge that made you focus on the needs of others (instead of your own). Describe that experience to the group. Do you Really Live more when you're focusing on your own needs...or on the needs of others? Why?

5. How do you tend to view becoming the person God made you to be? (Pick one)

- A single quest woven throughout my daily life
- One of many quests in my life
- Other _____

Now tell the group why you chose what you did.

» Group Bible Exploration

1. God calls each of us to live for something more than ourselves. Read together the words of Jesus in Mark 8:34:

> "Whoever wants to be my disciple must deny themselves and take up their cross and follow me."

Maybe you've heard these well-known words before—when Jesus invited his followers to "take up their cross." Do you wonder if the disciples really understood that Jesus was calling them to lives of sacrificial love and serving? When you hear this phrase—"take up their cross"—do you tend to view it as a burden or an opportunity...or both? Why?

2. Read Numbers 13:26–33, the account of the Israelite spies' report on exploring the land of Canaan. Here are the key verses:

> They gave Moses this account: "We went into the land to which you sent us, and it does flow with milk and honey. . . . But the people who live there are powerful, and the cities are fortified and very large. . . . Then Caleb . . . said, "We should go up and take possession of the land, for we can certainly do it." But the men who had gone up with him said, "We can't attack those people; they are stronger than we are. . . . We seemed like grasshoppers in our own eyes, and we looked the same to them." (vv. 27, 28, 30–31, 33)

How did most of the men respond to the challenges facing them? How did Caleb respond? What do you suppose allowed Caleb to have a different outlook? Do you think you would've responded the way Caleb did or the way the others did? Why?

As you think about your reaction to the spies' situation, consider whether you tend to be more of a fearful or fearless person as you face life. Which do you *want* to be? If you need some encouragement, here's a reminder from the DVD:

> The Spirit wants to make you a dangerous person. The Spirit wants to make you threatening to all the forces of injustice and evil and greediness that keep our world from Really Living. The Spirit wants to make you dangerously good in a broken world.

3. Read together, in Joshua 14:10–12, Caleb's statement made more than 40 years after he and the other spies first saw the land of Canaan:

> "Now then, just as the LORD promised, he has kept me alive for forty-five years...while Israel moved about in the wilderness. So here I am today, eighty-five years old! I am still as strong today as the day Moses sent me out; I'm just as vigorous to go out to battle now as I was then. Now give me this hill country that the LORD promised me that day. You yourself heard then that the Anakites were there and their cities were large and fortified, but, the LORD helping me, I will drive them out just as he said."

Decades after exploring the Promised Land, Caleb's hunger for following God in the midst of challenges was still there. Think about your own life: Do you feel that you're growing more open to the adventures that God's calling you to? Or do you more often shy away from God's nudges? Why?

Do you suppose it matters that Caleb was focusing on a cause bigger than himself? What about you—do you need to do any life "rearranging" to help you find a cause bigger than yourself?

4. Do you ever assume that other people who are facing a challenge probably are completely confident in their abilities? It's easy to presume others have what it takes and we don't. But read these words from the apostle Paul (an amazing New Testament leader) in 1 Corinthians 2:3–5:

> I came to you in weakness—timid and trembling. And my message and my preaching were very plain. Rather than using clever and persuasive speeches, I relied only on the power of the Holy Spirit. I did this so you would trust not in human wisdom but in the power of God. (NLT)

Do you see what Paul relied on to carry out what God called him to do?

Now read Paul's words in Romans 12:6–8:

> In his grace, God has given us different gifts for doing certain things well. So if God has given you the ability to prophesy, speak out with as much faith as God has given you. If your gift is serving others, serve them well. If you are a teacher, teach well. If your gift is to encourage others, be encouraging. If it is giving, give generously. If God has given you leadership ability, take the responsibility seriously. And if you have a gift for showing kindness to others, do it gladly. (NLT)

Which gift or ability is each person called to use when facing the mountain God has planned for him or her? What happens if each person doesn't choose to use his or her individual gifts? Now think about this—what could happen if *everyone* used their gift(s)?

Check out this passage from *The Me I Want to Be, Teen Edition*:

> How will you recognize your mountain? Well, there's no formula. Just like every other area of your growth, your mountain won't look exactly like anyone else's. But often you'll recognize it because it combines the stuff that you're best at with the stuff you care most about. Yet know this for sure: *God has a mountain with your name on it.*

Dream for a minute about what your mountain could be—what God is calling you to. Do you honestly believe there's one with *your* name on it? If you're open to it, share your thoughts with the group.

» In Closing

As you complete this final session, close in prayer. Ask God to help the group members see the challenges in their lives as opportunities for the Spirit to be at work. And ask God to give them courage to find their mountains and take a risk for God's kingdom. Celebrate what God has done in each person through the conversations in this DVD study.

Then encourage the group to keep following God's activity in their lives by completing the "On Your Own in the Coming Days" section (beginning on page 86).

» On Your Own in the Coming Days

It's easy to talk about being (and even *wanting* to be) the person God made you to be. But to actually put that desire into action means putting that pursuit above everything else. During this next exercise, you'll need to open your heart to God's call on your life to make a difference. Are you ready?

Take a risk and carve out some time to think through these questions and activities:

1. During the group discussion time, what logo did you choose for your life? If you didn't choose one yet, take some time for reflection and see what God might bring to mind. Once you have the logo in mind, draw it as best you can (no artistic skills required!). Then hang it up where you'll see it a lot. Let it remind you of what you want your life to be about—now and in the future.

2. Now consider the idea that God has a mountain—a challenge—specifically for *you*. Do you really believe it's true? Have you ever asked God for a mountain—*your* mountain? If not, what keeps you from asking God for one? If it's fear, uncertainty, or another reason that enters your mind, invite God to replace that reason with trust and courage. God can do that!

3. Next, write out some of your deepest passions, gifts, and desires—jot down whatever comes to mind. (And don't worry—it's not bragging!) Do you see any connections or patterns in the things you've written? If you feel stuck, ask a close friend or family member to help you recognize the passions, gifts, and desires in your life. Sometimes other people can really help by sharing what they see in us.

4. Now explore your "world." Is God already at work in any areas of your life where you might be able to use your strengths? In prayer, ask God to open a door, to show you the mountain or challenge God has for you. And when God gives you your mountain, go climb it!

As you get ready to close this book and lean into all that you've learned about Really Living and becoming the Best Version of you, remember these words from *The Me I Want to Be, Teen Edition*:

> Don't ask for comfort. Don't ask for ease. Don't ask for manageable. Ask to be given a vision for a challenge bigger than yourself—one that can make a difference in the world, one that needs the best you have to give (and then leave some space for God besides). Ask for a task that will keep you learning and growing and uncomfortable and hungry.
>
> Ask for a mountain!

Share Your Thoughts

With the Author: Your comments will be forwarded to the author when you send them to *zauthor@zondervan.com*.

With Zondervan: Submit your review of this book by writing to *zreview@zondervan.com*.

Free Online Resources at
www.zondervan.com

Zondervan AuthorTracker: Be notified whenever your favorite authors publish new books, go on tour, or post an update about what's happening in their lives at www.zondervan.com/authortracker.

Daily Bible Verses and Devotions: Enrich your life with daily Bible verses or devotions that help you start every morning focused on God. Visit www.zondervan.com/newsletters.

Free Email Publications: Sign up for newsletters on Christian living, academic resources, church ministry, fiction, children's resources, and more. Visit www.zondervan.com/newsletters.

Zondervan Bible Search: Find and compare Bible passages in a variety of translations at www.zondervanbiblesearch.com.

Other Benefits: Register yourself to receive online benefits like coupons and special offers, or to participate in research.